CW00457478

Market Research
in a week

Market Research
in a week

POLLY BIRD

Hodder & Stoughton

A MEMBER OF THE HODDER HEADLINE GROUP

As the champion of management, the
Chartered Management Institute shapes and
supports the managers of tomorrow. By sharing
intelligent insights and setting standards in
management development, the Institute helps
to deliver results in a dynamic world.

chartered

management

institute

inspiring leaders

For more information call 01536 204222 or visit www.managers.org.uk

Orders: please contact Bookpoint Ltd, 130 Milton Park, Abingdon, Oxon
OX14 4SB. Telephone: (44) 01235 827720. Fax: (44) 01235 400454. Lines are open
from 9.00–6.00, Monday to Saturday, with a 24 hour message answering service.
Email address: orders@bookpoint.co.uk

British Library Cataloguing in Publication Data
A catalogue record for this title is available from The British Library

ISBN 0 340 81150 1

First published   2003
Impression number   10 9 8 7 6 5 4 3 2 1
Year   2007 2006 2005 2004 2003

Typeset by SX Composing DTP, Rayleigh, Essex.
Printed in Great Britain for Hodder & Stoughton Educational, a division of
Hodder Headline Plc, 338 Euston Road, London NW1 3BH by
Cox & Wyman Ltd, Reading, Berkshire.

C O N T E N T S

You know that your customers like what you provide, but you want to make it better. Or maybe you've just had a brilliant business idea and want to know how it will stand up in the market. Perhaps your boss wants an assessment of the company's sales compared with its competitors. All these and many more questions can be answered by using market research.

Market research is an important marketing tool and one that many people are having to use for the first time. Whether you are the owner of a small business and want to do some market research yourself or you are an employee who has been asked to arrange some market research this book will help you. By understanding what market research is for and how it is used you can make sensible decisions about whether you need it and who will do it for you. If you do it yourself this book will help you do it better. Or if you are using a market research team it will make sure they are doing the job you want and answering the questions you need answered.

This book takes you through the main steps in market research and gives you the basics for following it up. During the week we will look at:

Sunday: *Market research – what it's all about*

Monday: *Planning the research*

Tuesday: *Types of research*

Wednesday: *Research methods*

Thursday: *Doing the research*

Friday: *Analysing the results*

Saturday: *Using the research*

You will achieve a basic understanding of what market research is about and how it works, and this will enable you to start putting the techniques into practice. This book won't confuse you with the details of such things as statistical analysis, although these are mentioned, because there are many more detailed books to help you. But you will have the groundwork for carrying out basic research or overseeing a market research project. By being aware of the problems and techniques you can ensure that the research you commission is done properly.

This book will be particularly useful to students who want an accessible overview, business people wanting to do their own market research or employees who have been asked to oversee a market research project for the first time. Anyone who wants to know what market research is will find this book helpful.

How you use this book is up to you. You might use it as a practical 'hands on' guide or as an introduction to a subject vital to today's commercial life. However, by the time you have read this book you will have a much better understanding of the importance of market research in business life.

Market research – what it's all about

Today we will examine what market research is, why you need it and who should do it. We will also learn about the main uses of market research.

- What is market research?
- Why should you do it?
- Who should do it?
- What are its main uses?

What is market research?

Any successful business needs to know who its customers and potential customers are and what they want. Without that information it is difficult to make decisions about what product or service to sell or where and how to target customers. Market research is a way of finding out this information using various research techniques. It provides people running a business with the information they need to make important decisions about the way that business works. It is generally used when there are specific problems or situations that need dealing with but where adequate information to make the necessary decisions is currently missing. For example, a decision might need to be made about whether to launch a product in a new country or whether to scrap a product entirely. Market research involves the collection of the necessary data which is then analysed in depth and presented in a report in a form that is easily understood.

Market research:

- Focuses on specific situations or problems
- Involves collecting information
- Results in analysis of data

Market research involves gathering relevant data by the most appropriate means. This is usually achieved by gathering information from a sample of individuals or organisations and can relate to their characteristics, behaviour, attitudes, opinions or possessions. It can also include research from sources such as consumer and industry surveys, psychological investigations, and observation or focus group studies. The specific methods for obtaining the information are discussed in more detail in Wednesday's chapter. The type of research undertaken and how long it will take depends on the particular problems involved. The methods used are specifically adapted to each new project. Because some research involves surveys of opinions rather than facts it is sometimes classed as a social science. Some of the research methods used are also used by social scientists. Research might therefore involve individuals, small groups of people such as households or companies and organisations.

Market research is the organised means of collecting, analysing, interpreting and presenting information to help inform marketing decisions.

Why do market research?

Every business has different reasons why market research would be useful. These vary with the problems each company has. You will know what problems need to be solved in your business. Generally businesses need to understand their customers and competitors and keep up with market trends and other aspects of the marketing environment. If you do not have enough information available to undertake a specific task or make a decision about an aspect of these areas then you might need market research to provide extra input. For example, you might need to find out why a particular product is not selling or whether it is sensible to launch a new product or service.

> You need market research to:
>
> • Reduce risks
> • Grasp opportunities
> • Improve results

There are three other very good reasons for doing market research. First, if you try to make a decision about a situation or problem without the correct or adequate data you will take much longer than necessary and may make an incorrect decision. You can't afford the time and money that would be wasted. By obtaining the correct data, properly analysed and presented in a form that you can easily understand, you can make an informed decision much more quickly and reliably. Second, your competitors will be using market research to improve their own performance. You risk getting left behind if you don't make the most of the information available to you. Third, the quality of information provided by good market research will be more accurate and detailed than any accumulated piecemeal from less informed sources. While intuition and experience are valuable they are not adequate for all situations and work better for being backed by detailed and accurate data.

You can also use market research to:

- Monitor and assess markets
- Judge market trends and conditions
- Find who your competitors are

The better you understand the markets in which your product or service is launched the more confidence you will have in your decision making and you will reduce the risks. Market research can help establish the need for a product or service, give a new or failing product a boost, and show what strategies you could use to move your business forward. You might have a long-term need, for example, monitoring market trends. Reliable data in this situation would help you plan an effective media campaign or reposition your product in the market. Or market research might be used in the short term, for example, to evaluate the success of a particular product over three months.

Who should do it?

Market research can be done by a number of different kinds of people:

- Yourself
- Group of staff
- In-house marketing team
- Professional market researcher
- Market research agency

If you have plenty of time you or your staff can undertake research for simple situations yourselves. Reading this book should help you plan and undertake a basic market research project. You might get a different group of staff together to do the research for each project. If possible, designate a particular member of staff to take charge of every project to provide continuity, preferably someone with training in market research methods. If you have a marketing department in your company it will be used to doing research and this book will help you provide accurate information to enable it to plan an effective project. For more complex situations you can pay a professional market researcher or a market research agency to undertake research for a specific problem. This is particularly useful when you need a continual supply of accurate and up-to-date data in a hurry. Professional market researchers, whether individuals or in agencies, can find, analyse and report back on data very quickly, usually much more quickly than you could do it yourself. If you use someone else to do the research this book will give you an understanding of what they are doing and help you monitor the standard of their work.

Throughout this book we will use two imaginary businesses as examples of market research techniques. Sally wants to open a SupaSnak sandwich bar in a small market town. Oddtaste Ice-cream Co. has the bright idea of introducing a new savoury tuna ice-cream to its customers and wants to know whether it will sell as well as its standard range.

The main uses of market research

Market research is useful in seven main areas of a business and can help resolve particular situations in these areas or be used for long-term monitoring of a particular problem. These are:

- Products
- Sales
- Customers
- Pricing
- Promotion
- Markets
- Distribution

Product

Market research can tell you whether the product is popular or not, and the reasons for this, whether a new product is likely to sell, what customers want of a new product, what faults there are in the product or proposed product and how it compares with others already in the market. It can also help with branding and communicating a new product and encouraging its acceptance.

Sales

This can involve tracking sales trends at company and individual retail level, monitoring sales of a particular product, forecasting sales. It can pinpoint retail needs.

Customers

Your customers might be organisations as well as individuals. You might need to know who they are, what they think of the company, product or service, how they view your competitors, what they want from your company, information about how customers are treated and how they think you could improve.

Pricing

You might use market research to find out whether a product or service is correctly priced, how your prices compare with those of competitors, how to price a new product or service, how to price special offers or deals. It can monitor the effect of changes in pricing structure and analyse past trends.

Promotion

Market research can be used to help you focus your promotional efforts on the right people and places, compete against your competitors' advertising, help you decide where your promotional efforts should be directed to get the best value for your money.

Several of these areas may overlap but market research can provide data that will help you focus on the right areas to achieve the best results. It can help you plan a media campaign, help creative development, help create sales plans and provide data on the media.

Markets

You use market research to find out the size of your market, who the main players are, help decide on branding and distribution, and discover what the market trends are and your position within them.

Distribution

You need to get your product or service to your customers and market research can discover what your retail needs are, whether they are being met, and show the best ways of increasing distribution speed and amount.

Another way of looking at market research is to think of it as focusing on three main areas:

- Your customers
- The market place/sales environment
- Your competitors

You need to have information about each of these areas to ensure that you are making the relevant decisions. You need to be able to target your customers so that you can focus your efforts on getting your product or service to them. The marketplace is the environment in which you have to pitch your wares. This might be influenced by economic, social or political forces. Being aware of these helps you keep up-to-date with the latest trends in your industry. You can also research your competitors to find out what is and isn't working in similar companies and get ideas for improving your own product or service.

Summary

This chapter has shown you that market research is a powerful tool for understanding your customers. When you know why market research is important and what areas of information it covers, you can choose the most appropriate people to provide the information. Effective market research needs to be well planned and executed and the following chapters will show you how to do this.

Tomorrow we will look at how to plan the research.

Planning the research

Today we will examine how to plan the research. We will also look at the importance of producing a written market research plan.

Stages in a market research project

Before you can plan a market research project you need to be aware of the stages it should go through. These are:

- Define the problems
- Develop hypotheses
- Collect the data and test the hypotheses
- Analyse and interpret the results
- Report the results

However, before these stages can be completed the project must be planned. Once the planning has been completed the other stages can be undertaken. Unless a market research project is planned carefully time and money can be wasted.

Planning a market research project

Careful planning is the key to a successful project. Do not skimp on the planning stage because it can help to eliminate unnecessary work.

Planning market research

- Define the problems – aims
- Choose the audience
- Decide what information you need
- Choose personnel
- Decide research methods and parameters
- Allocate resources (money, time)
- Ensure accuracy and quality
- Choose appropriate questions

Define the problems – aims

To be effective your research must focus precisely on the problem or problems that you need to solve. This means that you must decide what the aims of the research are. These can be arrived at by asking questions that need to be answered.

Sally wants to open her SupaSnak sandwich shop in a small market town in the Midlands. She defines her problems by asking questions which will provide guidelines for any research:

- Is there enough demand for sandwiches in the town?
- Who would buy them?
- What is the competition?
- What would be the best street in which to place a sandwich shop?
- Is the area up-and-coming, i.e. are there signs of retail growth?

The problems may include decisions you need to make or opportunities you would like to examine. Unless the research relates closely to these you will waste time and money on unnecessary work. Irrelevant research will also confuse the issues and you will waste resources on side issues which may be interesting but not relevant to the problems in hand. By defining the problems you can work out exactly what questions to ask to get the information you need. Examples of problems and opportunities involving products or services are:

- How to launch a new product or service
- Dealing with a low market awareness
- Problems of low use of a product or service
- Dealing with a company's poor image or reputation
- Distribution problems

To ensure that you plan your research to get the answers you need you must:

- Decide exactly which problem you want to solve
- Define the problem as precisely as possible
- Identify any subsidiary problems

Decide which problem

Every organisation has a myriad of problems that need solving. But to make sure that your research is effective you need to decide which of these problems is necessary and most important to deal with. Remember that urgent isn't the same as important. You need to decide which problems are important and, more importantly, which problems could be most usefully solved by using market research.

Oddtaste Ice-cream Co. wants to find out who buys its ice-cream and whether the new proposed tuna ice-cream would be popular with the 18 to 35 age group.

Once you have decided which problem can and should be solved by market research you need to define it as precisely as possible. By specifying the aims you ensure that any research is focused and exact and that unnecessary time, money and personnel are not wasted. Defining the problem carefully also allows the person who commissions the research to see whether the research is being conducted carefully. It also ensures that you can more easily determine what research needs to be done and in some cases how it should be done. For example, if you need opinions about your product or service rather than detailed figures, the research method would involve talking to potential and actual customers or doing a survey rather than analysing sales figures.

Identify subsidiary problems
Although generally you will want your research to focus on one problem there may be times when there are related problems that could be answered at the same time. If you identify any subsidiary problems you should ensure that they:

- Are closely related to the main problem
- Can be sensibly addressed during the market research to be commissioned
- Will not entail extra or irrelevant work

Ideally your market research should focus on one problem. However, if you think that one or more related problems

need to be tackled at the same time keep them to a minimum.
The more focused your research, the more accurate the
results and therefore the more use to you.

Developing hypotheses
Once the basic desk research has been done you should be
able to form some tentative hypotheses which can be tested
by primary research if necessary. These hypotheses will
dictate the questions that you ask.

An example of an hypothesis is 'that tuna ice-cream will
be more popular with the 18–35 age group than other
age groups'. The research would then test whether this
hypothesis was true or not.

Choosing the right questions
Once a market research plan has been created it will be
possible to formulate the questions that will be asked during
the research. These might be specific questions for interviews
or questionnaires, or questions to determine the research to
be done in books or on the Internet. Unless the problems
have been defined accurately these questions will be time
wasting or misleading.

Choosing the audience

How you conduct your market research depends heavily on
who it will be aimed at. The audience for market research
might be:

- You
- Managers
- Business partners
- Staff
- Product creators

The audience you aim at not only decides how the research should be conducted but what questions to ask and how it should be presented.

> The audience for Sally's SupaSnak research will be herself alone. For the Oddtaste Ice-cream Co. it will be the company's decision-makers, that is the senior managers.

Once the problems or opportunities to be researched have been identified and the audience for the results determined, it is possible to decide whether you need to have detailed answers to all the questions.

What information do you need?

Once you have defined the problem and decided on the aims, you need to work out what information you need to collect through market research that would help you solve the problem. This will involve deciding what information is needed to solve the problem. It is likely that having defined the problems and audience the aims will be clear, for example, to establish certain data, to discover the needs of a particular market or to provide enough information to tailor a product to a particular market. However, there may be less specific aims. You may, for example, simply want to examine the problem in greater detail so that you can define it further. Whatever the reason for the research, the more specifically you can define it the more accurate the results will be.

Collecting a lot of general information about the problem will not be a good use of time if you try to sift through a lot of irrelevant data. If you are commissioning the research from an outside agency then once you have agreed the main objective the market research team you employ will work out the most useful information. However, if you are doing it yourself or advising an in-house team you need to be aware of the following:

- Where the information will come from
- Who will provide the information
- The time allowed for collecting the information
- Whether the information is readily available or needs to be collected fresh

Specific research gathering techniques are discussed in detail in the following chapters.

You need to create a list of basic information that you need from the research. Write down everything you can think of but be prepared to tailor it to resources available to you. Time, costs and the number and expertise of the personnel available will restrict the amount and type of research that can be undertaken. With so much information available today you might experience 'information overload' and the information available may be too much to use in a particular project.

There are certain things you can do to make the search for information more manageable:

- List all the information you need
- Reduce the list according to the type of research you are doing
- Set limits to the research (e.g. geographical or demographical)
- List all the possible resources

Demographic = the way populations are structured

As the research progresses you may find that some of the results you get may make other research unnecessary. For example, if results show that a certain geographical area is unsuitable for a product launch then no further related work about that area is necessary. There is no right or wrong way of obtaining the necessary information but you will need to bear in mind that certain techniques are more appropriate for certain kinds of aims.

Choose personnel

To carry out accurate and reliable research you generally need qualified and experienced people. For example, anyone untrained in market research interview techniques risks introducing bias into interviews. If you are not using an outside agency then anyone doing market research in-house should be experienced or at least take advice from someone who is. It may be possible to arrange in-house or day-release training for a new market research officer. The number and type of personnel available to do market research will affect how long the project will take to complete and the costs.

Although generally one person working in-house can complete a small sample research by interviews, larger nationwide surveys are best left to outside agencies. Having said that, an in-house market researcher given the time and resources and a clear plan of action can achieve much.

Real life example

J.B. was asked to complete a nationwide survey of approximately 30 major companies in a production industry. He completed 30 individual interviews with the decision-makers in the industry nationwide as well as undertaking detailed desk research on all the companies. He completed the research and wrote up the report on his own in three months.

There is less of a problem about personnel if you use an outside agency because it will supply the necessary resources according to the project's needs.

Research methods and parameters

Once the aims and objectives of the research have been established you must decide how the information will be obtained. This will sometimes depend on how the results will be analysed. Most projects will start with basic desk research.

Desk research is research that can be carried out from one's desk by using the telephone, fax, a computer and books.

Money and time

Both time and money put restraints on any market research
project. These need to be allocated as part of the market
research plan from the start so that work can progress within
them.

Money
Your main restraint will be the cost of the research and this
will determine the main decisions such as who should do the
research and how long it can last. If large companies risk
losing a great deal of money, should they get their products
or service wrong, they will be willing to spend a lot of money
on market research. So a company with a huge turnover
might spend thousands of pounds on market research
because even if the results are unfavourable much more
money will be saved. One the other hand, the owner of a
small or medium-sized enterprise (SME) might allocate a
small amount of one year's profits for a small research project
or perhaps up to a tenth for a major project.

Market research costs must be budgeted for from the start
and be planned into the project from the beginning. Even if
you plan to do the research in-house you should calculate the
costs as if you were paying an outside agency. It is easy to
underestimate the costs of your market research if they are
not all included from the beginning. Once these have been
calculated it may be that buying research from an outside
agency works out cheaper in the long run.

Time
The time available for a market research project will be
limited by external company or industry deadlines as well as
the actual time needed to complete the research. In the end

the amount of time available for the project will be a
compromise between the actual time available and quality.
Any time allowed for the project must be realistic and take
into account any seasonal or other cycles. Also remember the
basics of project management and work backwards from the
desired end date when allocating time.

Ensuring accuracy and quality

Accuracy and quality are related concerns that must be
considered when planning any market research. Both affect
the legitimacy of the final data.

Accuracy
Before any market research can be undertaken you need to
decide what level of accuracy will be acceptable in the
results. This must be linked to how the results will be used as
well as how the data is collected. It is important to ensure
that the correct type of data is gathered according to the
degree of accuracy acceptable. Interviews, for example,
would not be acceptable if specific and highly accurate
figures were necessary. Determining accuracy is discussed in
more detail in Thursday's chapter.

Quality
Quality relates not only to the results but to the way they are
carried out. Research must be accurate if it is to be used to
make reliable decisions. On the other hand, poor research is
unreliable and misleading. The quality of data collection and
analysis must be strictly controlled, as must the organisation
and conduct of the research project. Using a reputable
outside agency or an experienced in-house researcher will

ensure this. If you want to take charge of the project yourself you need to plan it carefully and introduce checking procedures to monitor the quality. Do your best to validate the data and if possible be compare it to other similar independent data. However, as long as the personnel are experienced, the working practices are good and the stages of the project are checked carefully as it proceeds the quality of the research should be acceptable.

Writing the market research plan

Any market research plan, whether in-house or from an outside agency, should be written down in a clear and accurate form so that everyone involved understands what it will entail. An agency will produce a plan or proposal as part of its commission but it is also sensible to produce a plan for any in-house market research project. A written plan enables the work to be monitored and checked at regular stages and time and costs can be contained.

A plan should:

- Describe the problems
- Explain research aims and objectives
- Explain what information will be needed
- Describe research methods and how they will be monitored
- Indicate how the research will be reported
- Detail the time, costs and personnel to be involved

The plan will be a detailed and accurate account of the issues raised in the planning process and how the research will be carried out. A good market research plan is the basis of the research.

Recording progress

If you decide to do your own market research it is quite easy to lose track of where you get to with your plan. Unless you keep a check on your progress you might be spending too long on some parts of your plan and not enough on others. Or you might miss out one or more important steps. The most effective way to ensure that all parts of the plan get dealt with and to keep within financial and time limits is to keep a detailed record of your progress against your targets.

When you have written your market research plan, divide each stage into specific smaller steps. Assign each step a time limit and a named person to complete that step. Give a copy of the progress record to everyone involved in the project and keep a copy yourself. Personnel involved in the research should be told to use the progress record to ensure that they complete their assigned tasks within the stated time limits. Completed tasks should be recorded in the progress record. The project manager should check everyone's record weekly (or more frequently for a shorter or more critical project) and record it on the master record sheets. In this way gaps in the research will be quickly spotted, as will cases where progress is too slow. Keeping detailed progress records of the research enables mistakes to be corrected and will provide a blueprint for further research projects.

Summary

Today we learnt that it is important to plan a market research project carefully and that there are specific stages to go through before a research project can begin. We know that:

- To create a good market research plan you must define the problem accurately and be clear about the aims of the project
- There must be hypotheses to be tested
- You must decide the audience for the research as this determines the questions and methods to be used
- The project will have constraints of money, time and personnel
- Accuracy and quality must be built into the research methods
- A written plan is vital to formalise the project plan and to act as guidance for the project.

This chapter has described the methods for creating a usable market research plan. The following chapters will show you how to put this plan into action and carry out the research.

Tomorrow we will look at the different types of research and discuss the pros and cons of each.

Types of research

Today we will and look at the differences between quantitative and qualitative research and examine the different methods of research, including primary and secondary research. We will also discuss the main sources of secondary research.

Quantitative and qualitative research

Market researchers divide their research generally into two kinds, *quantitative* and *qualitative*. These two kinds of research dictate not only how the research is carried out but who the respondents might be and the form of presenting the results.

What is quantitative research?
Quantitative research is based on careful measurement of aspects of the market such as market size, distribution levels, sales trends and so on. It aims to produce data that can be statistically analysed and expresses the results numerically. The results need to be reasonably accurate so the researcher must use methods that can achieve this.

> *Quantitative research*
>
> Quantitative research is the accurate measurement of aspects of the market which produce results that can be statistically analysed and expressed numerically.

What is qualitative research?
Qualitative research is based on understanding what people feel, think and understand about products and services. It

usually deals with information that is too difficult or expensive to quantify numerically. The researcher aims to understand consumer attitudes to a product or service and what needs are being satisfied and why and how. This type of research uses methods and ideas borrowed from the social sciences. It is usually achieved by interviewing individuals or during group discussions.

Sally will be conducting some simple quantitative research. The answers to her questions to a specific number of people will provide her with numerical totals that she can analyse.

Oddtaste Ice-cream Co. needs to find out whether young people would like the idea of tuna ice-cream. It will do some qualitative research and interview young people to find out their views on odd tasting ice-creams.

The pros and cons of quantitative and qualitative research

Although these two research methods are widely used they each have a number of advantages and disadvantages. A researcher must decide at the start of any research which type of research should be used. This will inform the methods of research and the importance of the results.

Quantitative research is sometimes cheaper if the data is already available. However, costs will increase if you have to employ experts to analyse the results. Qualitative research has the advantage that smaller samples can be used and non-quantifiable data such as attitudes can be obtained. However, it can be expensive although there are some less accurate kinds of qualitative research that can be done cheaply. It is also more prone to bias than quantitative research because of the attitudes and training of the individual interviewers.

Other aspects of research

There are other aspects of research such as the differences in the time span during which the research is undertaken, that is:

- continuous
- ad hoc

Continuous research

This type of research is undertaken regularly and continuously over a long period of time and is useful for showing trends. So, for example, regular research about a product's sales might be done by a large organisation in order to discover seasonal or other variations.

Ad hoc research

Ad hoc research is research undertaken to provide answers to a particular problem that needs to be dealt with quickly. This type of research is concentrated and of short or defined duration.

Primary and secondary research

The two main methods of research are *primary research* and *secondary research*. Primary research is information that is obtained first hand, that is, new information. Secondary research is information that has already been collected by somebody else. In this chapter we will discuss the basic sources for secondary or desk research. Primary research will be discussed in detail in the next chapter. Primary research can be qualitative or quantitative while secondary research is more often quantitative.

Primary (field) research
Primary research involves researchers obtaining new information first hand. Because it involves contacting other people and usually involves going out and about it is also called *field research*. This research brings the researcher into direct contact with the consumer, product or service. It is usually carefully designed to ensure that individuals or groups provide enough material for analysis. Field research is undertaken by researchers who go out to the public or who test the product or service in its setting. So this type of research might include interviews, group discussions, shop visits, or product testing by the public.

Secondary (desk) research
Secondary research is the means of obtaining information that is already in existence or which comes from a third party. It is also often called *desk research* because, as the name implies, it can often be completed from the desk of the researcher using printed information, the Internet, the phone and so on. The information might be internal, that is, available within the researcher's own organisation, or external where the information comes from elsewhere.

Pros and cons of secondary and primary research

Secondary research has many advantages over primary or field research. It may answer all your questions without the need for primary research and so make the project cheaper. It can be used to guide the amount and type of primary research required and so save time and money. However, it may be out-of-date or inaccurate or there may be simply no relevant secondary material available. It is often not in the form required for the project.

Primary research has the advantage of being up-to-date and the accuracy can be controlled to some extent. It can focus on the exact questions you need answered, and by careful preparation of the method of collection can be collected in a form which makes analysis easier. Unfortunately it is prone to bias unless carefully monitored and the cheaper methods may be less reliable.

Which type of research first?
For most projects it is sensible to conduct preliminary desk research and then on the basis of this decide whether further research should be primary or secondary. Secondary or desk research is quicker and cheaper than primary research. It also ensures that research already available is not repeated and so saves time in the long run. In some projects the restraints of time and budget will make desk research the only viable option. However, secondary research cannot provide all the information. For example, up-to-date consumer attitudes can only be obtained through fieldwork.

Where both primary and secondary research is used in order to provide as complete a picture as possible then this is *omnibus* research.

Recording your research

Whether you are doing secondary or primary research you need to ensure that you have arranged a reliable method of recording the results before you start. We do not yet live in a paperless world and even in this age of computers market research generates a great deal of paperwork. This needs to be dealt with methodically. Make sure that paper is stored in readily identifiable files so that it can be found again easily and quickly. Similarly, if you use a computer to record research it must be stored in suitably named and easily accessed computer files and folders.

During secondary research use a standard method of recording notes and storing photocopies. Be sure to record:

- The original source of the data
- The date the data was created
- The data's creator(s)
- Who can give permission for its use (if necessary)
- Where you found the data (this includes website URLs)
- Date you accessed the data (to judge how out-of-date it is when you next look at it)

For primary research much of the recording will be done on standard forms such as questionnaires or specially designed forms for notes when following a scripted interview or making observations. Transcriptions of tape recordings must be stored in the relevant folder or computer file and the tapes labelled and stored in a suitable container. This good housekeeping with recording and storing your data will ensure accuracy and enable you to easily check the origins and results of any data.

Obtaining secondary data

Many market research projects start with an analysis of available data by desk research. In this chapter we will look at how to obtain this secondary data. Most companies rely heavily on the use of secondary data. Not only is it cheaper but it is usually more quickly and easily obtained. It has the advantage that someone else has done the work of collecting it but it may be scattered and in an unsuitable form for your use.

Where to look for secondary data
Secondary data can be found in a great many places but falls broadly in two categories, that is, *internal* and *external* sources.

Internal records
Before you use external sources you should first see what you can obtain from within your own organisation. If you are using a market research agency it should be given access to any internal records. They will also use their own secondary resources. You should look first to see what is available in the way of previous reports on the subject or similar subjects, any publications they may have produced, previous data written up as reports, comments from in-house experts and practitioners and so on. These may point the way to external secondary sources. You will probably find more than you expected. Sometimes overlooked and seemingly unexciting documents such as internal accounts can be particularly useful. You might find these sources useful:

- Sales records
- Information about past activities
- Research reports
- Accounting records
- In-house magazines and newsletters
- Customer surveys
- Information about competitors

You should then look at any books such as directories or statistical reports that your organisation holds and talk to in-house experts. Only when you have exhausted the internal sources should you turn to external sources.

External sources
The Internet is often the first place researchers start. But be careful. Just because it is a popular research tool it doesn't mean that you will find everything you need there. It is rarely enough to use online searching on its own. There are a number of basic sources for secondary research that any market researcher should try:

- Libraries (external)
- Company data (other companies)
- Directories and almanacs
- Books of statistical data
- The Internet (including online databases)
- Academic research
- Media articles in the general and trade press
- Reports by data agencies
- Commercial sources e.g. sector reports
- Trade and industry associations
- International sources
- Government databases e.g. statistics, reports, census, indices

- Directories of sources
- Industry experts
- Industry data e.g. abstracts, statistics, directories
- Market research reports
- Unpublished sources

As you can see there is a great deal of readily obtainable secondary information, much of which can be accessed from your desk via the Internet or the phone. Unless you are only going to undertake primary research you should try these sources first. In fact, much research will be started by extracting relevant information from these sources before any primary research is considered. Some market researchers specialise in obtaining and presenting secondary data.

Other companies' records
A lot of information is available from other companies, such as their annual reports, sales figures and so on. This is often made available to the public from the company's web-page. If the information is not there the site may tell you how to get the information in printed versions.

Directories and almanacs
These can provide data on their own or point the way to other data or organisations where data can be obtained.

Books of statistical data
There are many books which provide data on a wide range of subjects. It is unlikely that you will be able to use the data in exactly the form it is presented but it can provide the basic numerical data.

The Internet
The Internet is a huge worldwide source of information. However, as anyone can put information on the Internet you need to check that the source is reliable. The most reliable sources are generally government, company and academic sites. Check that the information is up to date (see when the site was last updated), who posted the information (an individual or organisation) and whether there is contact information. There are a lot of commercial organisations that provide detailed data and statistics online. These usually charge either a subscription or one-off fee for accessing the information.

Academic research
Academic research is available in the form of books, articles in the general media and academic publications, reports posted on the Internet and by approaching relevant academics at universities and colleges who may be willing to share their findings.

Articles in the general media and trade press
Virtually every trade and industry has its own magazine or newsletter and articles on trades and industries are published every day in the general media. These vary from detailed industry reports with lots of data to general articles. For a full list of UK or international media consult the relevant volume of the annual *Willings Press Guide*.

Reports by data agencies
Data agencies produce their own reports and sets of data and these are usually available for a fee or subscription.

Commercial sources e.g. sector reports
These are reports and data produced by fee-paid
organisations. They may be available in book form or on CD.

Trade associations
As well as their own journals trade organisations produce a
great deal of information about their own sectors and
organisations. Their addresses can be found in yearbooks such
as *Whitakers Almanack* or Hollis' *The Directory of UK Associations*.

International sources
Like their UK counterparts there are international directories
and yearbooks giving information, data and the names of
organisations which could provide it. You can also search for
the websites of international companies on the Internet.

Government databases e.g. statistics, reports, census
Governments produce statistics and reports on a wide range
of subjects. Some of this is available free of charge, either in
print or on the government website; some must be paid for.
An important starting point for much desk research is the
demographic information provided in the UK government's
census reports.

Directories of sources
Directories give names of organisations that can provide
information or suggest where it can be obtained.

Industry experts
Often the easiest way of getting information is simply to
phone someone and ask them. Use academic or industry
directories to find the expert you need and contact them
directly with specially prepared questions. Be polite and be
prepared to phone back at a time more suitable to the expert.

Industry data
Most industries have data compiled for their own use and may make this available to market researchers, perhaps for a fee. You can contact them through the industry organisations as mentioned above.

Market research reports
Other market research organisations may make their data available for a fee.

Unpublished sources
These may be unpublished academic research or research by organisations that has not yet been published in any form.

What next?

After the basic desk research has been done you can decide whether primary, or further secondary research should be the next step. You need to decide:

- Whether it should be mostly qualitative or quantitative (i.e. do you need quantifiable data or opinions?)
- How large a sample the information will be obtained from
- How the data will be collected
- How the data will be analysed

The answers to these questions will be determined by costs, time, acceptable accuracy and the research objectives.

Before doing any field research you might need to supplement your secondary research with interviews (which are primary research) from people such as:

- The sales staff
- Former directors
- Buyers
- Trade and industry journalists
- Newspaper editors
- Stock analysts
- Competitors and former competitors
- Independent industry pundits

Checking reliability of sources

Just as you need to be careful about the reliability of information on the Internet, you also need to be careful when using printed sources. Books, articles, statistics and directories can all be less reliable than you expect. Do not assume that facts presented in articles or books are correct. Use the most up-to-date version of any collection of statistics or directories.

Generally, you can assume that some sources are reliable. Information from government sources, academic institutions and well-known commercial organisations are likely to have recorded information accurately because they have reputations to protect. If you are uncertain about how reliable a source is, check the reputation of the author and how recently the work was produced.

When accessing a source's reliability you need to know:

- Authorship – was it produced by a well-known and generally reliable source?
- How up-to-date it is – use the most recent version of any directory, statistics, company report etc.

- How detailed it is – specifics are more useful than generalisations.
- Author's track record – has this author or organisation produced other respected work?
- Reason for creation of source – was it produced for a specific reason that might make it biased, or is it likely to be neutral?

If time allows use two or three separate sources to cross check facts and figures.

Summary

Today we have explored the difference between quantitative and qualitative research and learnt the pros and cons of each. We have looked at secondary and primary research and discovered the many sources for secondary research. We have learnt that:

- Quantitative research uses data that can be numerically quantified
- Qualitative research provides information about attitudes and behaviour
- Secondary research can be done from a desk with a telephone and a computer
- Primary research requires first hand observation or questioning of people
- There is a vast range of secondary sources and the Internet is one of the most important

Tomorrow we will look at the basic primary research methods.

Research methods

Today we will examine basic primary research methods and how to use them. We will look at the pros and cons of these methods and how to choose the most effective for the job you have to do.

Primary research methods

Be careful not to waste time doing primary or field research that can be readily found by desk or secondary research.

There are many primary research methods available. You should understand how each of them can be used but not all of them are suitable for all research projects. The main types are:

- Interviews
- Surveys
- Hall tests/central location tests
- Focus groups
- Panels
- Mystery shoppers/store checks
- Observation
- Diaries
- Real-time tracking

Interviews
- *Face to face interviews*. These are flexible although the questions can be standardised. However, these can be time-consuming and costly and difficult to design. Visual aids can be used. More highly structured longer-lasting in-depth interviews can be used to obtain more detail.

Interviews can take place in the street, in a neutral place or in respondents' homes. Nowadays the most common interview type is the pavement interview where a percentage of people who pass a certain point or who fit a certain profile are interviewed in the street. An interview conducted in the home might last from 45 to 90 minutes. Doorstep interviews are much shorter.

- *Telephone interviews.* Interviews can be conducted by telephone and are usually recorded on tape for transcription and analysis later.

Surveys

Surveys are questions posed to a selected sample of people. The questions are usually standardised and this enables a large sample of people to be questioned. Bear in mind that some people prefer to answer questions in person while others prefer to write them down. These are the main ways of conducting a survey:

- *Postal surveys.* These are popular because they require fewer staff to administer and are therefore cheaper. They can also cover a much wider geographical area. They can be sent to respondents on paper, computer disk or fax. However, you can't tell who is going to complete the form and questions are more easily omitted. There may be a low response to postal surveys and some people may take a long time to reply. Postal surveys may be followed up by reminders. 40% is a good response from a postal survey and with two reminders this can by increased to as much as a 78% response
- *Telephone surveys.* These are quick and low cost but there is less rapport with the respondent and they may suspect the interviewer of trying to sell something. Usually a selected

list of potential respondents is used but many may not be at home or refuse to reply. However, where the person does answer the phone the response rate is usually higher than mail surveys.

- *E-mail questionnaires.* These are quick to administer and cheap but there is low security and anonymity can't be guaranteed. There is also a high level of non-response. However, the popularity of going online means that they are now widely used and can be useful.

- *Computer-aided telephone surveys.* These involve a touch-screen computer to enable respondents to complete a questionnaire and the data is collected and tabulated very quickly. A laptop can be used to take the questionnaire to respondents.

- *Web-based surveys.* This is another quick and cheap form of survey where questionnaires are loaded onto a website and visitors to the website are invited to complete the questionnaire. Such surveys are usually used to collect quantitative data. Online research has the potential to reach a great many people worldwide. Unfortunately the sample is self-selecting because not everyone has access to the Internet and nor will everyone who accesses the website complete the questionnaire, unless you have a pre-screened panel of respondents. So web-based surveys may often not be representative of the general population.

- *Pavement surveys.* A certain number of people chosen by specific criteria are stopped in the street and questioned. This has the advantage of obtaining an immediate response from interviewees but relies on the researcher being able to find enough people with the desired characteristics willing to stop and answer questions.

Sally decides to use pavement surveys to collect quantitative data by interviewing a certain number of people during the lunch hours of Monday to Saturday. She prepares a list of five questions with simple multiple choice answers. She will also record the sex of the respondents. The results can be added up and compared and will show how popular the idea of a sandwich bar will be.

Hall tests/central location tests

These are interviews that usually take place in a hall, room or other central site close to a shopping centre. Selected people invited by telephone or using the shopping centre are invited to the hall where they are asked about a product. These types of test are most often used to evaluate new products themselves but they can also be used to get opinions on such things as advertising, the price, the product name or the packaging. A suitable hall or room is hired for a day and adequately staffed and the products prepared beforehand. If a sample of 500 or more people is needed then the same tests may take place in several towns. These tests are useful when the questions concern sensitive issues that respondents may not wish to discuss in public. Hall tests can be expensive because they are costly to arrange because of the costs involved in arranging such things as hall fees and incentives to those taking part. However, the expense may be justified by the effectiveness of the results.

Focus groups
A focus group is a group of six to ten people brought together, usually informally, so that the researcher can

observe their interaction to an idea or concept. You will have
to decide what criteria the members of the group should
have in common. The questions can be structured or
unstructured but the discussion as a whole needs to be
controlled. The session may last from one to two hours. The
advantages of these groups is that they are quick and cheap
and non-verbal communication can be observed. You may
find that people are more honest than if interviewed alone.
But there is the danger that one or two people will dominate
the discussion or that some people will simply agree with the
majority view. Some people may become too embarrassed to
speak in a group situation. Also the small sample can mean
that the group is unrepresentative of the wider population.
The success of focus groups depends very much on the skill
and personality of the researcher who must be sympathetic
but objective.

Odd taste Ice-cream Co. decides to use focus groups
to obtain views on the proposed tuna ice-cream. They
will invite ten people in the chosen age group in six
cities to give their views.

Panels
Panels are groups of people who have agreed to provide data
either when asked or on a continuous basis for organisations
such as government bodies, commercial firms, academic
institutions and similar. They might be asked to provide
consumer, retail, industrial, audience data or complete home
diaries or audits. Sometimes they might be asked to come
together as a focus group but often supply the data from a

distance through questionnaires. Depending on the scope of your research you might organise a panel group of your own or obtain the information from an outside agency.

Mystery shoppers/store checks
This type of research involves researchers entering shops incognito to observe or to ask specific questions to test certain retail procedures. For example, a mystery shopper might pretend to be a customer to see how polite the sales staff are or how well they deal with a specific enquiry. Someone doing a store check might look at which products are on display in a particular area of a store. Some of the research may be done by telephone, for example, to test how well follow-up enquiries are dealt with or how fast phones are answered. The aim is to find out what really happens at the practical end of a business. These kinds of checks are generally reliable and can be used to encourage good staff. But some staff might be concerned that they are not given the chance to withdraw from such checks and that their anonymity might be compromised. Also the sample of stores and staff might be small. In the end the success of this type of research depends on a mystery shopper's expertise.

Observation
Some primary research is done by observation rather than by dealing with the people directly. This may be done by simply noting behaviour, for example, how many times people use a certain cash machine, or by using technology such as cameras, tape recorders or other devices. This method can be useful but might be compromised if the people being observed become aware of the researcher and this could lead to bias in the results.

Diaries

Use of diaries involves a group of respondents, either a regular panel (see above) or specially selected for a particular piece of research, to keep a diary. For example, they might be asked to record their television viewing habits or daily activities. The advantage of this method is that it is an easy and cheap way to collect data but the disadvantage is that it relies heavily on the honesty of the diary writers because there is no way of checking whether they have been recording their entries truthfully. Also it involves time and commitment on the part of the writers and this may cause people to drop out of the research.

Real-time tracking

Real-time tracking needs commitment by researchers. It involves evaluating performance of aspects of a business over a period of time. This is measured at regular intervals, for example, daily, weekly, monthly or quarterly, and reports are produced regularly. It can provide an up-to-date view of customer reactions and enables a business to resolve any problems as quickly as possible. It involves a lot of planning and researchers need to be able to reach possible respondents quickly. It also takes a long time to arrange.

Choosing the right method

It is important to use the right method for your research. This will depend on whether you are gathering data that can be quantified or whether you want qualitative results. Methods that lend themselves to data collection that can be quantified include:

- Surveys
- Online data collection
- Observation

Methods that relate to qualitative research, that is collecting opinions and attitudes, are:

- Focus/panel groups
- Hall tests/central location tests
- Mystery shoppers/store checks

Like all research you should know what it is that you want to find out and then choose the most appropriate method of collecting the necessary information.

Pilot study

If you intend to carry out a large survey you might find it worthwhile to conduct a pilot study if you have time. A pilot study needs to be large enough to provide a useful indication of whether a full size survey would provide worthwhile results but small enough not to use up all your resources for the actual survey.

Designing a questionnaire

The most common tool for primary research is the questionnaire. This can only be correctly designed once you have decided the aims of the research. The questions must be designed to be strictly relevant to the research. A good questionnaire must be:

- Impartial
- Clear
- Easily understood
- As short as possible
- Designed to collect only the information you need
- Exclude offensive questions
- Leave room for detailed answers
- Have an inviting layout

You need to decide:

- The size and length of the questionnaire
- How much to explain
- Number of questions
- Type of questions
- Wording of questions
- Layout of questionnaire

Before you start

Before you design your questionnaire or survey you need to decide exactly how you are going to conduct the questioning and how the surveys will be completed. You need also to decide what interviewing or survey techniques you will use, for example, face-to-face interview, phone survey, pavement survey, and how to record the results. Unless you decide this before you plan your questionnaire it may be inaccurate and be subject to avoidable practical problems. When this has been decided you can then design your questionnaire or survey to take these practical issues into account. Examine as many examples of questionnaires as possible to get an idea of how yours should be designed.

The types of questions

There are two main types of question you can use:

- *Open-ended*. For example: What do you think of this product? These are more time-consuming and harder to analyse than other types of question but can reveal more.
- *Closed/structured*. The respondent chooses from a given set of questions. These might be:
  - *Dichotomous* (given a choice between two contrasts). For example: Do you drive a car? Yes? No?
  - *Multiple choice*. For example: Are you aged between (a) 0–15 (b) 16–30 (c) 31–45 (d) 46–75
  - *Scales*. Respondents are asked to record their answers on a scale (perhaps from 1 to 5 where 5 is the most agreement and 1 the least).

Most questionnaires use a mixture of question styles. Be consistent. For example, place answer choices on the same side of the page each time otherwise the respondent may get confused. Always test your questionnaire before you use it to iron out any misleading questions or spelling mistakes.

Summary

Today we have learnt what different primary research methods market researchers can use and the pros and cons of each. We know that:

- Primary research can be used to collect quantitative and qualitative data
- Questionnaires, interviews, observation and mystery checks are the main primary research methods

- Questionnaires are the basic tools of most primary research
- Questionnaires must be impartial and carefully worded

Tomorrow we will look at how to do the research.

Doing the research

Today we will examine how to choose a sample. We will
learn how to determine the sample size and how to deal with
questions of bias or non-response (i.e. incomplete data). We
will consider the question of privacy and the implications of
the Data Protection Act in Market Research.

Defining your population

You must first decide what comprises your population. You
then need to define it by the individuals, groups of
individuals (e.g. households) or other units (e.g. companies).
It is normally further defined by geographical extent and the
time over which the research will be carried out. This defined
population is your population frame. Normally your
population will be your target market. Beware of making
your population too narrow otherwise you may miss
possibilities. However, too large a population would be too
costly to use.

Next you need to decide whether to carry out a census or
take a sample.

Census
A census includes all of the population, for example, every
person in the UK or all of your customers. To conduct a
census of even a limited population is often ruled out
because of the amount of time and money such a study
would need. For example, Sally couldn't ask everyone in her
market town whether they would use her sandwich shop nor
could Oddtaste Ice-cream Co. ask every person in the UK

whether tuna ice-cream is a good idea. However, sometimes the information you need is available in a ready-made form such as the UK national census.

The disadvantages of using a census is that it would be very expensive to conduct research on this scale and it could affect the result. For example, if you asked everyone in advance whether they would like a particular new product you would lose the element of surprise when the product was launched. However, there are occasions when using a census would be useful and practical as long as the population was of a manageable size. So a small business that wanted to get an accurate description of what its customers thought of it might ask all its customers for their comments.

In market research:
- *Population* = all the individual members or parts of a group that a researcher wants to study
- *Population frame* = your population defined by type of individuals or other units, geography and time
- *Sample* = a section of a market research population selected to represent an attitude or characteristic of the whole population
- *Census* = using the whole population instead of a sample

Choosing a sampling frame

If you decide to use a sample, you need to remember that your information is only as good as the sample you choose. Your sample must be relevant and representative of your target population. The large size of most populations (whether of individuals or other units or elements) means that it is usual to choose a part of it to represent the whole. Most market research is based on a sample representing the whole population. The selection might be made on any number or kind of criteria, such as age, sex, income, geographical location, and so on. So Oddtaste Ice-cream Co. might sample people based on age, perhaps 18–35. The decision to use a sample rather than a census is usually based on considerations of time, cost, accuracy and the likelihood of substantial bias. A list of individuals or other units in your population from which your sample will be drawn is called a sampling frame.

> *Sampling frame* = a list of individuals in your target population frame, for example a list of customers

Your sampling frame restricts the population to a manageable sample but may not represent all the population. In theory you can define your population before choosing your sampling frame. In practice it is easier and more usual to choose a suitable sampling frame first and use it to define the population. Your sampling frame must not be so rigid that it excludes necessary units, nor so loose that it includes too many irrelevant ones.

A sampling frame must therefore:

- Ensure that each person or other unit appears only once
- Ensure that there are no omissions
- Include all the chosen population
- Be up-to-date and accurate
- Be easily accessed

Typical and easily available sampling frames include such things as the telephone directories, post office postcodes and electoral rolls.

Pros and cons of easily available sampling frames

There are some commonly used large sampling frames. Their advantages are that they are fairly easily obtained, relatively cheap and require no compilation on the part of the researcher. However, they do have some disadvantages.

Telephone directories
The telephone directories provide an easy sampling frame, being widely available in libraries or on CDs. The sampling frame is likely to be reasonably wide because most people have a telephone. However, they are incomplete because not everyone has a telephone and you cannot tell how many people use the same telephone at one address. Some subscribers may be ex-directory or, especially in the case of businesses, recorded twice under variations of their name.

Post Office postcodes
These cover all the UK and provide an easily accessible demographic. There are sources of demographic information about postcodes that will enable you to decide which area would be most suitable for your research. If you are looking for a sample based on a geographic area then this is a useful source. You might choose a wide area or a postcode representing a smaller area within that. However, the individual postcodes usually represent several houses in a street and therefore it is difficult to estimate the number of

people you will be sampling. However, if you want a sample of a particular geographical area and are intending to send out questionnaires then this is a good way of doing it. However, there may be omissions as there is no way of telling whether people have moved on.

Electoral rolls
These used to be a very good sampling frame as they recorded the names and addresses of everyone over the age of 17 who would be over 18 and eligible to vote in the forthcoming election. They are available at Post Offices and libraries. However, the Data Protection Act means that there are now rules regarding privacy and that many voters can now opt out of having their details revealed to people with no legitimate reason to obtain them and that includes market researchers. This means that available voting lists are no longer complete for public viewing. The information is also always several months out-of-date.

Customer lists
If you are researching customer opinions then a relevant customer list can be a good sampling frame. However, some customers may be omitted and the list will not generally contain past customers unless it is out-of-date, nor will it be able to provide details of potential customers.

If you cannot find a relevant sampling frame for particular characteristics readily available, such as ice-cream eaters, you will have to question people until you have enough willing interviewees for a sample.

Sampling accuracy
Accuracy in a sample can be affected by sampling and non-sampling errors.

- *Sampling error* = an error in the selected sample itself such as choosing a non-representative sample
- *Non-sampling error* = errors in how the data is collected or interpreted

If you use a census, non-sampling errors can be increased because of the large amount of data. In a sample these are reduced and if the collection is carefully monitored they can be more carefully controlled. So generally using a sample for market research is better. A sample of the population is also less likely to affect the attitudes of the population as a whole.

Choosing a sampling method

You next need to decide how to extract your representative sample. You can do this by two methods: *probability* or *non-probability sampling*.

Probability sampling

Probability sampling uses statistics to enable a researcher to make generalizations about a population from sample results. Everyone in the research population has a known chance of being chosen at random. If a few people or units have an unknown chance of being selected for the sample then the sample will be biased. It means that there is a way of working out the degree of confidence that one can have in the results. There are a number of probability sampling techniques. The basic techniques are:

- Simple random sampling
- Stratified random sampling
- Proportionate and disproportionate stratified random sampling
- Cluster sampling
- Multistage sampling
- Area sampling
- Random walk sampling

Simple random sampling

A sample chosen by this method uses random numbers from books of random number tables or generated by computer. You first define your population and get a sampling frame, that is, a listing of all the individuals in your population, for example, a customer list or electoral roll. A sampling interval is calculated by dividing the population by the required sample size and selecting a number at random between one and the sampling interval. Using that as the starting point every number counted at the sampling interval is selected until the required number of the sample is chosen. This is used to choose units from the sampling frame. All the units in the sampling frame have the same chance of being selected.

Stratified random sampling

The population is divided into groups according to common attributes or characteristics. For example, a sampling frame of footwear manufacturers might be divided into large, small and medium companies. Then each group or stratum is subjected to random sampling. The idea is to ensure that the groups of population in the sample comprise the same proportion of the population as they do in the whole. There is the risk with this method of omitting important segments of the population.

Proportionate and disproportionate stratified random sampling
Proportionate stratified random sampling ensures that the sample has the same proportion of a certain attribute as the whole population does. With disproportionate stratified sampling this is not the case.

Cluster sampling
With this sampling technique the population is divided into subgroups or clusters. Each group is as alike as possible in certain characteristics but different from the other subgroups. So all the units are included but the clusters do not overlap.

Multistage sampling
This is one of the most commonly used sampling methods when a random sample of the whole population is needed. It is like cluster sampling with an extra stage included. Only certain clusters are sampled. Samples of subgroups within clusters are chosen at each stage until individual units are reached and then these can be selected as a sample. It can be usefully used where at the lowest level there is no adequate sampling frame. The trouble with this method is that because it covers such a large population the sampling error is increased.

Area sampling
This is a kind of cluster sampling where geographical areas are chosen as the subgroups. A random sample is made of the areas and then of the individuals within the selected areas.

Random walk sampling
This approximates to random sampling. Interviewers are given random starting points but specific routes to follow and fixed rules about which individuals or houses/flats/other buildings to approach.

Although it is useful to know what these methods of probability sampling involve many of them are too complicated and specialised for a non-expert to use with confidence. Unless you are going to choose a sample by using simple random sampling or random walk sampling the process is best left to experts.

Non-probability sampling

In these techniques the chances of an individual or unit being selected are unknown and this reduces the ability to generalise about the population as a whole. Because no sampling frame is needed these methods are cheaper and they are often chosen because they are convenient for the researcher. They can be useful but only if done well, otherwise the results can be worthless.

Non-probablity techniques include the following:

- Convenience sampling
- Judgement sampling
- Purposive sampling
- Quota sampling
- Snowball sampling

Convenience sampling
You choose a sample chosen simply because it is convenient for you.

Judgement sampling
This is a sample chosen by someone with relevant expertise or experience and which is based on their knowledge.

Purposive sampling
In this case you might choose a sample not because it represents the population as a whole but because the people have specific attitudes or characteristics which would make the research a success.

Quota sampling
A sample is chosen which has a characteristic in the same proportions as the whole population. Interviewers are told to select people according to two or three criteria, such as age, sex or hair colour. This is prone to interviewer bias in who they select and the subgroups may need adjusting to better reflect the population.

Snowball sampling
This is a random sample based on the recommendations of people interviewed. After being questioned themselves respondents are asked to recommend others to take part in the research, who then suggest others, and so on. The sample is therefore self-selecting but it can be useful if the researcher is looking for unusual characteristics.

Deciding whether to use a probability or non-probability sample

Whether you decide to use a probability or non-probability sample will depend on the aims and expectations of your research. If you want to be sure that the sample reflects the population, that error can be calculated and the probability known, then you will choose a probability sampling technique. On the other hand, if you want a sample that is convenient, cheap, but possibly unrepresentative of the whole population and more prone to sampling error, then a non-probability technique will be useful. Cost might be a deciding factor as non-probability techniques are cheaper. You also need to take into account how costly an error in the results would be.

Choosing a sample size

Once you have chosen the method of sampling you need to decide how large your sample should be. If the population is largely alike then you can use a smaller sample. But if there is a large variation in the population then you will need a large sample. Remember that for some methods you will need to divide your sample into subgroups or clusters. You will not be able to analyse these subgroups accurately unless the sample size is large enough. Accuracy does not depend on how much of the population is in the sample but whether the sample is really random. If the sample is truly random then smaller samples can be used.

The sample size also depends on:

- The required level of confidence
- The required level of accuracy
- How many people to allow for non-response
- The minimum number required to answer any particular question
- The practicalities of time, cost and personnel

In quantitative research the sample numbers are likely to be large (500+) while in qualitative research they may be much smaller (30 or less). The smaller number in qualitative research are because answers for each member of the sample must be analysed in detail and are often collected and considered by only one or two people. Sometimes research using a sample between these two extremes can by either quantitative or qualitative, depending on the type of research required.

Before you decide on your sample size ask yourself the following questions:

- What are the time, cost and personnel constraints?
- Is the aim quantitative or qualitative?
- What required level of accuracy do I need and what sample number will achieve this?
- Can I get the amount and type of quantitative data necessary?

Bear in mind that choosing a sample by one method may be costly but save money in the long run if the resulting information is accurate. One way of deciding a sample size is to compare your project with similar projects. You can also simply use your own judgement about what would be a suitable sample size. The cost of the project might determine how large your sample can be. The statistical method you intend to use for analysis might also determine the size.

There are a few generally accepted guidelines. For example, if you are using stratified random sampling or quota sampling then a minimum of 30 units in a group of people with particular characteristics (a cell) is usually required. The total number of units required for a stratified sample can be calculated by multiplying together the number of variables (characteristics) in each attribute required. For example, if you want to use people with three different hair colours, two heights and in four counties you would multiply $3 \times 2 \times 4$ to get 24. This would be multiplied by the minimum cell number of 30 to get 720, namely, the number of individuals to be questioned.

Sampling error

We need to know how accurate our research is likely to be. Typically in market research we work to a 95% confidence level. This means that we are looking for results that are 95% likely to be true, or if we do the research 20 times then 19 times out of 20 we will get the right answer. To find out the accuracy of a result we need to know the sample size and the results of the research.

Sample accuracy
To find out the accuracy of a sample:

- Choose the sample size (e.g. 400)
- Do the research or estimate the result (e.g. result is 170/400)
- Express that measure as a percentage (e.g. 42.5%)
- Take the percentage away from 100 (e.g. 100 – 42.5 = 57.5) and multiply this number by the original percentage (e.g. $42.5 \times 57.5 = 2443.75$)
- Divide this by the sample size (e.g. $2443.75 \div 400 = 6.12$)
- Take the square root of this answer and multiply it by 1.96 (e.g. $2.47 \times 1.96 = 4.8$)

In this example this means that in 19 times out of 20 you will get a result that is within 4.8 percentage points of the true result. In other words you are 95% confident that the proportion of the population as a whole is between 38.5% and 47.2%. Clearly if you want a more accurate sample than this you need to increase the sample size.

Problems of bias or incomplete data

Bias

Bias is a problem throughout market research. Bias can be in the sampling frame due to omissions, duplications and date. Sampling needs to be complete, accurate, representative and up-to-date. Desk research needs to ensure that data is accurate, complete, relevant and up-to-date. There are many ways in which bias can occur in market research through errors in the process. Errors can occur in the sampling method itself, the questions used or the way the interviews are conducted. Another problem which can affect the results is the non-response of some of the sample.

Non-response

If some of the chosen sample do not respond then the validity of the results may be reduced. This can be a very common problem in market research. Non-response means that the sample may then be too small to be representative or that a particular segment of the sample is not represented.

It is possible to deal with this in two ways.

- *Supplementary sample*. A second sample can be selected and the results added to the first results.
- *Trend analysis*. Results are predicted by projecting assumed responses from the respondents onto a graph.

Respondents' privacy

Now that the Data Protection Act (DPA) is in force it is very important that you understand the issues of respondents' privacy. Usually if a survey does not require any contact details from the respondent there is no problem with using the data. However, when you need to obtain and keep contact details, for example for follow-up surveys, the DPA must be taken into account. Permission must be obtained from each respondent for the research organisation to hold personal details and a guarantee given that this will not be used except for the purposes of the research and that the respondent will remain anonymous in any subsequent report. If contact details are held respondents have a right to see this on request and to have them altered or omitted. For full details see the DPA website on www.dataprotection.gov.uk

Safety first

Increasingly the message is getting through that everyone must be safety conscious. That applies just as much to market researchers dealing with the public. When organising market research in-house basic safety rules should be in place for anyone interviewing the public in the street, halls or people's houses. Ensure that all your researchers working in public follow these rules:

- Researchers should be assigned specific routes or spots and their whereabouts and times of work should be recorded before they leave the office
- All researchers should carry a mobile phone
- Female researchers should work in pairs
- No lone researcher should be asked to interview people in their own homes
- Somebody should be assigned to check at regular intervals on researchers doing public interviews or surveys
- Researchers should not be asked to work after dark or in locations in which they would feel unsafe

Researchers themselves should:

- Be courteous to the public
- Not take up more of the public's time than necessary
- Not hassle people who do not want to take part in the research
- Keep in touch with their office
- Not take unnecessary risks with their own or the public's safety

Summary

Today we have seen how to choose a sample and discussed the different sampling methods available. We have looked at the ways bias and errors can occur in the results. We have drawn the Data Protection Act to your attention and shown how the research can be conducted.

Tomorrow we will look at how to analyse the results of the research.

Analysing the results

Today we will examine the basic skills necessary to analyse the results of your research findings.

Why analyse the data?

You now have a great deal of data. What do you do with it? Raw data on its own won't answer your questions. Whether it is a collection of numbers or answers to questions it needs to be put into a form that can be used by both the researcher and the client who commissioned the research. To do this you need certain skills both in preparing the data for analysis and doing the analysis itself. Also, much of the analysis will be presented in report form. In the next chapter we discuss the best way of writing the report and what it should contain.

What skills do you need?

Unless the analysis is done carefully the results will be worthless. You need to have:

- Understanding of the project's aims
- Accuracy
- Objectivity
- Skill in preparing the data for analysis
- Skill in analysis
- Report writing skills

If you do not feel confident about your ability in any of these areas you should leave these parts of the research to other people. Professional researchers can deal with all stages of the research including analysis and report writing. Do not try to analyse the data yourself if you are unsure of any part of it otherwise you risk misrepresenting the results. If you want to keep the work in-house you should make sure that the data collection and the analysis methods are kept as simple and straightforward as possible.

What type of analysis?

Before carrying out any data collection you need to know what kind of analysis you will be doing. This will affect the data collection methods you use. You can't, for instance, use sophisticated statistical analysis using non-probability data. Try to use the use data collection techniques that will provide the easiest relevant method of analysis. You might do this by taking care over content and design of the survey or questionnaire. Also, remember that the results are for a particular audience and this might also affect how complicated the analysis needs to be and how detailed its interpretation.

Both quantitative and qualitative data can be analysed statistically but some qualitative data does not lend itself to statistical analysis and needs to be written up in essay report form.

Types of analysis

A simple table of responses from closed questions will produce a simple table of percentages. But it is usually more helpful to compare responses from different groups of people, for instance, distinguished by age, occupation or other characteristics. To get the most from the data market research analysis compares variables. There are two commonly used types of analysis that can be done using the data collected. These are *cross analysis* and *multivariate analysis*.

Cross analysis

Cross analysis is the comparison between two or three variables. This is the basic form of analysis and enables researchers to pick out attributes for particular sections of the population.

Multivariate analysis

Multivariate analysis is the cross analysis of more than two or three variables. It is harder to do but the complex statistical operations involved can be done on a computer. It is useful for finding out what is happening in specialist or niche markets. This is important because a lot of marketing today is based on segmentation. It is useful for statistical forecasting as it links the variable being forecast to other variables. It aims to represent the key characteristics of a market and how they relate to each other. Multivariate analysis can use attitude scales to show how brands are seen in relation to each other. This is called creating a *brand map*.

Where scalar questions have been used in the questionnaire these are used as attitude variables. The response can be groped into like segments using either *factor analysis* or *cluster analysis*.

This kind of complex analysis is best left to experts.

- *Factor analysis* = attributes in answers reduced to components
- *Cluster analysis* = describes attitudes of respondents

Graphs and charts

Although tables are the basis for market research analysis the results can also be presented in graph or chart form if they are straightforward. These can often give a more immediate impression of trends or proportions than tables. However, they are generally only suitable for less complex analysis.

Analysing quantitative data

All secondary data was once primary data. Before you analyse it you should check how reliable it is likely to be by going back to the source, if possible. Obviously this must often be taken on trust if the data is large or the source reliable, such as the government census. If there seems to be some doubt about the data try to compare two different versions from different sources so that omissions or errors can be noted.

Once you have accumulated and verified the secondary data you need to look for relationships, links and patterns which knit the data together. These patterns can point the way to other subjects and therefore other data.

There are certain steps to be gone through when analysing quantitative or numerical data whether obtained by primary or secondary research. Before analysis can take place the data must be put into a suitable form and one which is as accurate and reliable as possible. That is:

- Editing the questionnaires (where used)
- Coding the questions (where necessary)
- Putting the results into numerical form
- Tabulating the data
- Checking cross analysis (cross variable) tables
- Sorting into descending order
- Classifying into intervals
- Grossing up the sample to represent the whole population
- Analysing the results
- Reporting the results

Editing questionnaires
Where quantitative data is derived from questionnaires it is not safe to use questionnaires without checking them for accuracy. Each questionnaire must be checked for:

- Completeness
- Missed questions
- Whether answers are compatible

Many people fail to answer all the questions in a questionnaire and this has to be noted. Also check that the correct questions have been answered and that replies don't contradict each other. This checking process is done by hand. You can infer answers from the other answers given in the questionnaire where this can be done logically. Once the questionnaires have been checked the data in them ceases to be 'dirty' and becomes 'clean'.

Coding the questions
Sometimes questions are open-ended. The answers to questions like this are grouped into predefined similar groups. These groups are then coded and the code written

next to the relevant questions in the questionnaire. They can then be analysed by the usual methods. The problem with coding is that a lot of it depends on the judgement of the researcher and errors are more likely to occur.

Putting the results into numerical form
The basis of analysing data (unless it is qualitative data to be used in verbal form) in market research is to reduce the data, however collected, into numerical form. The data you have needs to be translated into percentages before it can be used. At its most basic this means adding up the scores from your data and writing them as percentages of the total sample number. It is usually not useful just to put the data in the form of raw numbers, for example: The number of women with red hair. It is usually more useful to put the numbers in percentage form, for example: The percentage of women with red hair in the sample is 12%.

When dealing with the responses to scalar questions the replies are often presented by using *mean scores* (the average of a set of numbers). Each answer is given a weighting number e.g. +1 for good, 0 for no opinion, –1 for bad. The score for each response (i.e. the percentage of the answers) is multiplied by the weighting number for that question. The total minus scores are then subtracted from the total plus scores and the answer divided by 100. Although this can be a useful way of reducing data to manageable proportions it needs to be interpreted carefully. Weighting a response may also be done if one characteristic is known to be over- or under-represented in the sample.

Useful words:

- *Scalar* = questions based on a scale of values
- *Mean score* = the average of a set of numbers

Tabulating the data
However the data is obtained it needs to be put in the form of tables so that numbers can be easily understood, for example, proportions or percentages. This can either be into the form of simple tables, that is presenting the results of one variable or using cross tabulation. This means that the relationship between two or more variables are put into table form. The person in charge of the project must decide the kind of tables to be produced and the data is then put into that form. Sometimes a special computer program will be written to do this; generally existing spreadsheet software can be used.

Checking cross variable tables
Cross analysis tables must be checked to see that they conform, that is that the number make sense within them and that the tables are in the correct physical form.

Sorting into descending order
Once the tables have been produced the results can be sorted into descending order and separated into groups relevant to the research. This too can be done by analysis software.

Grossing up the sample to whole population
Various statistical means are then used to gross up the sample so that it equals the whole population. This book is not the place to discuss these methods in detail. There are many good books that will give you the necessary information. But once these have been calculated the results can then be interpreted.

Analysing the results
Once you have put the data into tables you will need to
interpret them using statistical techniques. This is to
discover what is typical or not typical, that is, what is the
average result and how the rest of the results vary from this.
Analysing the tables shows how wide the range of
responses is and how the responses relate to the variables
being researched. At a basic level you will be comparing
percentages with each other. So for example if Sally
questions 50 people and discovers that 76% of them would
use a local sandwich bar and that 84% of them buy their
own lunches she might conclude that SupaSnak had a
future. Or if Oddtaste Ice-cream Co. discovered that 63% of
under 25s in Birmingham hated the idea of tuna-flavoured
ice-cream but that 45% also enjoyed popcorn they might
well decide to sell their traditional flavours in the local
cinemas.

Analysing trends is another aspect of analysing the results. If
you conduct your research over a period of weeks or months
you can plot the results on a graph. By plotting two separate
trends you can see whether there is any correlation between
the two. A growing trend towards ice-cream eating
correlating closely with a trend for eating next to rivers might
point to providing ice-cream vans along river banks.

Reporting the results
The results of the analysis are no good to anyone unless they
are communicated to the people who need to know, for
example, the people who commissioned the market research.
Once the analysis has been completed it must be written up
in report form and presented in a way that makes sense and
is useful to the client. It is on the basis of this report that the

client or other decision-makers will make decisions that will affect future action. Along with tables and graphs (e.g. pie, line etc.) you need to put clearly into words what the results show you. You also need to explain how the results affect the company and the consumer. (See Saturday's chapter for more information about writing the report.)

Make sure that you include details of the sampling error for your data (see Thursday's chapter on how to calculate this) so that readers can assess the accuracy of the results.

Adjusting the data

The sample to be analysed must be representative of the population but sometimes the sample does not do this well enough. It is therefore legitimate to weight the sample so that it is representative. This is done by multiplying a variable by a 'weighting factor' and this is put in a separate column – a 'weighted' column.

Qualitative data analysis

As we have seen the questions for qualitative data are usually more open-ended and the samples smaller. The resulting data can be more complex and contain more varied and possible meanings than quantitative data and analysis of it needs to be done with care. Some of the techniques available for quantitative analysis can be used for qualitative analysis but if this is done some of the useful detail might be lost.

Analysing qualitative data
The steps in analysing qualitative data are:

- *Transcribe the responses (e.g. taped interviews or written replies).* Transcribing from tapes can be tiring, time-consuming and often boring. If you ask someone else to transcribe a tape for you, you will need to ask the interviewee's permission for reasons of anonymity and confidentiality. Transcripts should be coded so that the subject can't be identified and kept in a safe place. You may need to change names and places for purposes of anonymity or if there would be any risk of repercussions.
- *Arrange for the results to be analysed.* Qualitative research results are usually analysed by the researcher. But if you do not feel confident to do this then you should arrange for a professional researcher with the relevant skills to do so.

Although qualitative research can be used to provide quantitative data this is more difficult and subjective to do. Much of the advantage of qualitative research is that it allows the respondents to reply at length and give their views. These views need to be gathered together in similar sections, for example, reasons given for wanting a sandwich bar in town, and the results written up in an essay type report. The analysis would therefore concentrate on explaining the similarities and differences in the replies and describing what this means for the company. Because the responses in qualitative data can be so varied it calls for skilled staff to make the final analysis. Unlike in quantitative data it is permissible to quote from the original responses in the final report. Often the analysis will be in verbal rather than numerical form.

Summary

Today we have looked at the basic methods of analysing the raw data. We have discussed the various kinds of analysis that can be done on the raw data and the procedures for analysing both quantitative and qualitative data.

Tomorrow we will look at how to use the research.

Using the research

Today we will look at the uses to which you might put your research and how best to present your research. At the end of the chapter we will find out where to go for more advice.

Uses for the research

The data as analysed has two important functions:

- Reducing uncertainty
- Keeping decision-makers better informed.

By interpreting the data decision-makers can make decisions based on reliable and up-to-date information. The better informed they are the more reliable their decisions will be and the quicker they will be able to make them. This reduced uncertainty means that there are less nasty surprises when decisions have to be taken.

Using the research to decide long-term strategy

The importance to you or your clients of market research is that it can be used to decide long-term strategy. Because of the time scales involved continuous market research is often necessary to keep up-to-date. Without the analysis of reliable data there is the risk of making expensive and dangerous mistakes that could have been avoided. It is the importance of forecasting long-term trends that gives market research its importance in today's market.

SWOT analysis

Simply reading the report through will not always give you enough information to make decisions. You need to take a proactive look at it so that it becomes a useful tool for decision-making and future action. One way of doing this is to analyse it by using SWOT analysis. This is a tool for pinpointing certain areas that need improvement or which otherwise need to be looked at. It looks at four main areas of a business – Strengths, Weaknesses, Opportunities and Threats.

Strengths
The report should show which areas your company excels in and which aspects of your product or service are doing well. If the research was analysing a particular trade sector it should show where the market was strongest. It will show which parts of the business attract customers and are performing well.

Weaknesses
Similarly the report will highlight where the business has a weakness. This will enable you to improve and amend this aspect before it gets worse. It will show what aspects of your business put off potential customers.

Opportunities
The report may indicate hitherto unconsidered areas of opportunity for the business. An early indication of this through market research might give you a head start in the market against similar businesses.

Threats
An analysis of the market can show where your business is being threatened by rivals or disenchantment by customers. Again, early warning of this may save your business.

SWOT analysis finds Strengths, Weaknesses, Opportunities and Threats.

You can design your research methods to answer these questions or the results may become clear when you analyse the data afterwards. By looking specifically at these four areas in the results you have a blueprint for improving your business.

Other important areas to look at include:

- Improving customer satisfaction
- Improving customer awareness
- Changing the product or service

Improving customer satisfaction
The more you know about what your customers want, the better you can produce the service or product that appeals to them. Market research can pinpoint the flaws and good points of what you offer as well as forecasting how well it will do in the future. It can help you target your customers accurately so that the people who want or need your product or service are the ones who receive it.

Improving customer awareness
Another important aspect of the analysed data is to show how well customers know about the service or product you are offering. This is an important step in deciding what kind of media campaigns and advertising need to be obtained to raise customer awareness.

Changing the product or service
Unless you know how well the product or service works or whether it is suitable for the intended customers you cannot

adjust it. By analysing suitable data obtained by market research you can pinpoint the changes that need to be made. This kind of research is ongoing so that you can continually improve and adjust your product.

Ethical standards

It should go without saying that market research should be carried out in a professional, reliable and honest manner. Unethical practices can lead to the results being unreliable or invalidated and seriously affect the confidence of the data. By ensuring that you maintain strict standards during the research and by using reputable researchers or market research agencies you will ensure that the data you use will be reliable. Researchers should:

- Maintain the anonymity of respondents
- Be honest about the data or its interpretation
- Not manipulate market research techniques
- Not alter research data
- Respect respondent's privacy
- Disclose sponsorship
- Admit on errors and limits of data
- Not disguise advertising as market research
- Avoid plagiarism

Dealing with the research results

Once the results of the research have been analysed and the report has been produced you need to decide several things:

- Who should receive the research
- The form of the research
- Where to deposit it
- How to distribute it

Who should receive the research
To maintain your business edge over your competitors you will not normally want to reveal detailed and possibly costly research beyond the decision-makers in your company. However, conclusions drawn from the report or actions based on it might be communicated to various other people and organisations where this would be useful. For example, you would want to let staff know about any new procedures which have been decided as a result of the report. Or a production manager might need to be informed about planned changes in the product or service. Although you would not reveal results in a promotional campaign the data might inform an advertising campaign so that it can be pitched at the most responsive audience.

Some simple research is done more as a joke or as part of a publicity campaign. So a questionnaire sent to 100 dog owners in Bradford might conclude that 75% of dog owners buy coats for their dogs. This could be used as the basis of a press release. These types of surveys are often used as a method of getting a company's name into the press even though the research may be limited or flawed.

You should also be clear about who not to send it to. It might, for example, be sensible not to send it to certain sections of the media who might misinterpret it.

The form of the research

Once you have decided who should receive the report you need to decide how it should be presented. Should you produce a full report, the summary, the conclusions or perhaps certain sections? If so, who should receive what? It is not always appropriate to send the whole printed report to everyone on your recipient list.

Where to deposit it

Market research is often referred to for many years after it was originally compiled. You should therefore ensure that it is placed somewhere readily available to authorised personnel. This might include the company library or company archives as well as the offices of certain decision-makers.

How to distribute it

Once you have decided the above points you will need to decide how to distribute it. Nowadays a written report is not the only form available. It could be presented as a CD or video presentation, a personal presentation as a talk or on a laptop, or as a printed document. The cost of producing the report and the time-scale you are working to will determine the form. A printed version is usually produced in any case.

Results are often also given to the commissioning clients (or other people in your company) in the form of a presentation. This can be done by using audio-visual techniques to demonstrate the main findings and recommendations. The written report should contain this information as well as any other relevant detail. This is where the graphs and tables come into their own. They can be shown in the presentation along with illustrations.

The final form of the report should be such that the vital information is easily accessed and understood. Even if the information is for your own benefit you will find it easier to understand and it will clarify your thoughts to have it in a suitable report form.

Remember your audience

It is important to remember for whom you are writing this report. If you are producing it for a technically sophisticated audience then the level of statistical detail can be much higher than if it is for non-technical clients. Bear in mind that most people will prefer a clear and straightforward analysis which can be easily understood and which makes decision-making quicker and easier. Clients will prefer to be able to interpret the findings without too much technical explanation. The amount of space and complexity given to research methods, procedures and detail of the data gathered should be tempered to the knowledge and expectations of your audience.

Bear in mind that the analysed data will rarely answer all the questions you have asked of it but it should answer the most important ones. Remember that even negative answers are useful.

Writing the report

There are many good books that can tell you how to write reports clearly and accurately. But here it is relevant to know what should go in one. The way the final report is written up will vary depending on who it is aimed at and the amount of details required from the analysis. However, there are also some logical needs for the report. It needs to be:

- *Simple but complete.* Answers can get lost in complicated analysis, but include enough detail to answer the questions.
- *Clear.* It needs to be easy to read so use straightforward language.
- *Accurate.* No grammatical or typographical mistakes which can change the meaning.
- *Short.* Even if the calculations are long the results should be presented in a short form. Use tables, graphs, charts and illustrations.
- *Follow a logical structure.*
- *In a user-friendly form.* Use headings and subheadings and provide an introduction, conclusions and an executive summary.
- *Answer the research questions as far as possible.*
- *Relevant.* Stick to the point.
- *Forward thinking.* Provide recommendations and action points.
- *Attractively presented.* Use a clear type face and include graphics, graphs, tables, illustrations, and so on.

Parts of a report

Different research projects and different researchers will produce reports in slightly different ways. However, a basic report should include:

- Cover page naming the authors of the report and the date
- Contents
- Executive summary

- Introduction – why the research has been carried out
- Main body of the report – the results
- Analysis – what the results show
- Conclusions – what the results mean for the clients
- Appendices

Learning from the research

Once the research has been completed, reported and seen by everyone who needs to know about it, how else can you use it? If you have done the research in-house it can be a useful learning tool for future market research projects. Once it is completed you should ask the people involved:

- What did we do well?
- What didn't succeed?
- What aspects could have been improved?
- Was there anything we could have done more quickly/ more cheaply/more efficiently?
- How good were our records/promises of anonymity/ questionnaires?
- Were the results we obtained complete/accurate/ unbiased/clearly presented?
- In what other ways could we improve our next market research project?

Remember that the people who have done the research are the best people to explain how effective it was. Make a note of any problems and suggestions raised by your market research team so that you can plan future market research projects better.

Where to go for more advice

This book has given you a brief outline of how to conduct market research. There are many market research agencies you can use. Look for those registered with the British Market Research Association (BMRA) at www.bmra.org.uk. The BMRA keeps a list of market research companies. Individual market researchers can be contacted through their professional organisation the Market Research Society (MRS) at www.mrs.org.uk. Other sources of information include the government and commercial companies.

Summary

Today we have looked at how to use the research including how to write the report and where and how to distribute it. By following the guidelines in this book you should have an understanding of market research and be able to plan, conduct and report on a market research campaign.

Did you enjoy reading this?
Do you want more time to learn new skills?
Why not try our new Six Weeks To range:

- ## MARKETING EXCELLENCE:
  includes: Marketing Plans • Viral Marketing • Building a Brand • Direct
  Marketing • Free Publicity for Your Business • Consumer Behaviour
  isbn: 0 340 81261 3 Price £15.00

- ## FIND A JOB
  includes: Planning Your Career • Job Hunting • Writing Your CV
  • Succeeding at Your Interview • Tackling Interview Questions
  • Assessment Centres and Psychometric Tests
  isbn: 0 340 81259 1 Price £15.00

- ## STRATEGIC EXCELLENCE
  includes: Business Strategy • Staff Retention • Operations Management
  • Total Quality Management • E-Business Strategy • Business Recovery
  Planning
  isbn: 0 340 81260 5   Price £15.00

- ## PROFESSIONAL EXCELLENCE
  includes: Project Management • Negotiating • Time Management
  • Dealing with Difficult People • Presentation • Memory Techniques
  isbn: 0 340 81262 1   Price £15.00

LEARN MORE FOR LONGER WITH SIX WEEKS TO
visit us at www.inaweek.co.uk

SUN

MON

TUE

WED

THU

FRI

SAT

For information

on other

IN A WEEK titles

go to

www.inaweek.co.uk